CREATIVE  TOUCHES™

THE HOME DECORATING INSTITUTE®

Copyright© 1996 Cy DeCosse Incorporated 5900 Green Oak Drive Minnetonka, Minnesota 5534.
1-800-328-3895 All rights reserved Printed in U.S.A.

Library of Congress Cataloging-in-Publication Data Valances etc. p. cm. — (Creative touches)
Includes index. ISBN 0-86573-998-6 (softcover) 1. Valances (Windows). I. Cy DeCosse Incorporated. II. Series.
TT390.V35 1996 646.2'1 — dc20 96-15847

CONTENTS

Getting Started

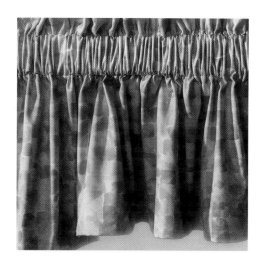

Rod-mounted Valances

Board-mounted Valances

Valances
ETC.

Almost any existing window treatment, from blinds to pleated drapes, can be enhanced with the addition of a stylish valance. If desired, a valance can be used alone on a window that requires no light control or privacy. A well-proportioned valance helps define the window, bringing it into the room's decorating scheme. When made of fabric that coordinates with wallcovering or furniture, the valance becomes a unifying element in the room.

Valances may be functional as well as decorative. They often hide unattractive drapery hardware at the top of the window. Board-mounted valances also serve to keep dust from settling on the undertreatment and block light from entering the room at the top of the window.

There are valance styles to blend with any decorating scheme, from country to contemporary. Some valances are mounted on rods, either by means of a rod-pocket or with decorative rings. These may be easily removed, if desired, for cleaning. Valances that are board-mounted can be freshened occasionally by vacuuming. All of these valances are easy to make and install, following step-by-step instructions with full-color photography.

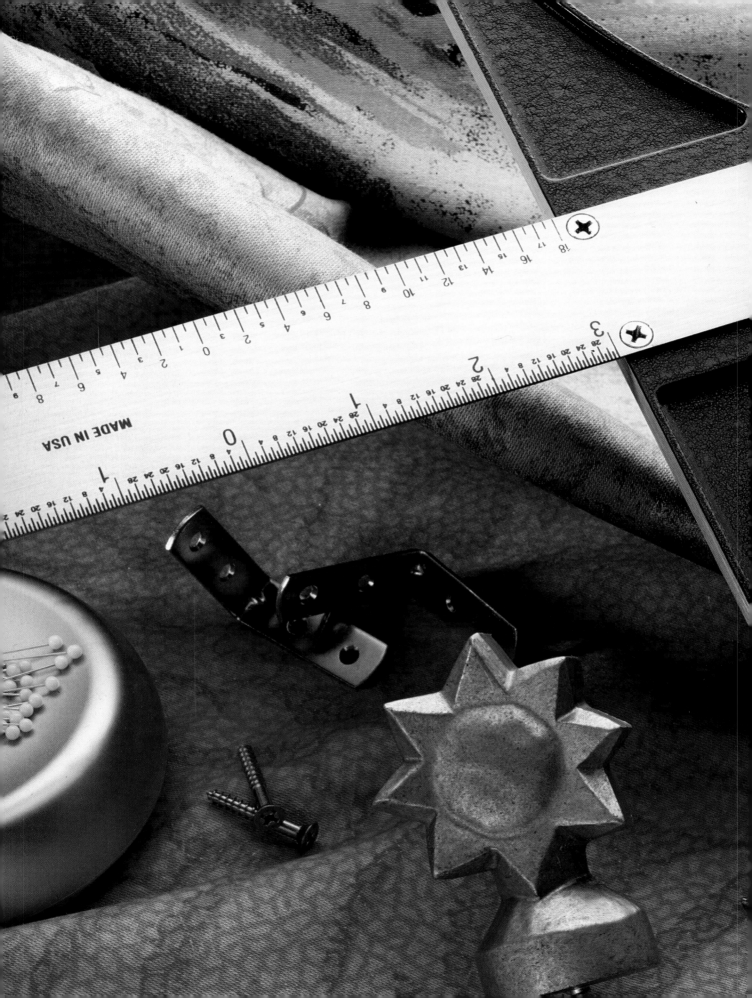

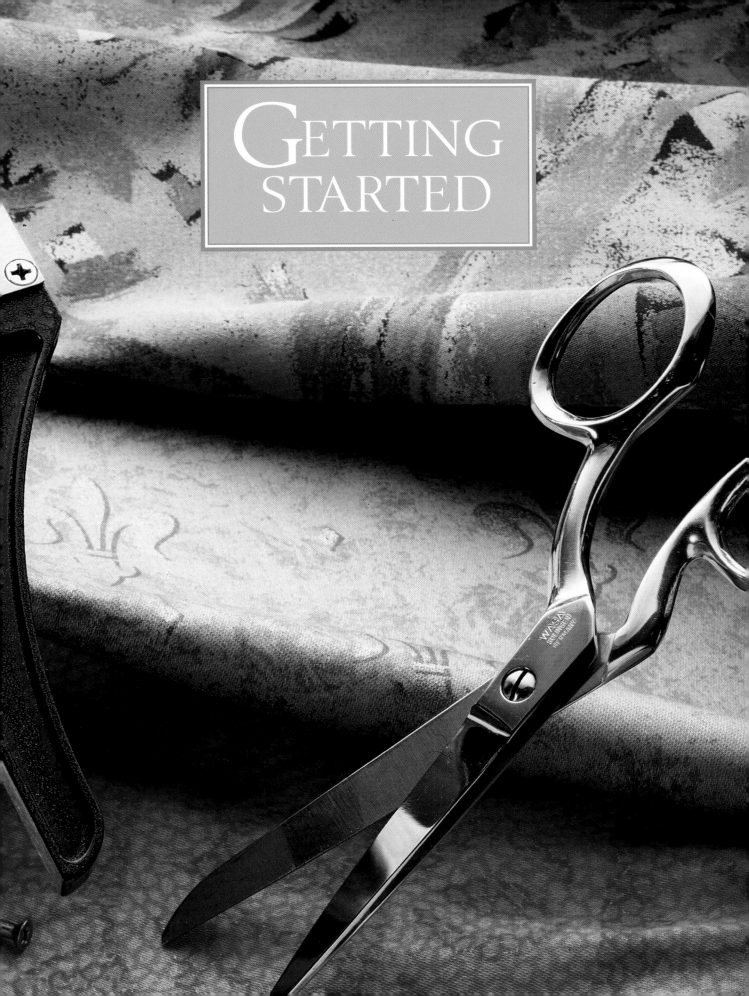

GETTING STARTED

Selecting & Installing Hardware

A

B

C

D

E

F

Careful selection of the hardware is essential to the success of a window treatment project. Decorator rods, pole sets, and decorative accessories enhance window treatments and are available in a variety of colors, finishes, and styles.

Window treatment hardware is packaged complete with mounting brackets, screws or nails, and installation instructions. Use screws alone if installing through drywall or plaster directly into wall studs. When brackets are positioned between walls studs, support the screws for a lightweight treatment with plastic anchors in the correct size for the screws. If the brackets must support a heavy window treament, use plastic toggle anchors in the correct size for the wallboard depth, or use molly bolts. If nails are supplied with the hardware you purchase, use them only for lightweight treatments installed directly to the window frame. Otherwise, substitute screws or molly bolts that fit through the holes in the brackets.

Curtain rods, available in several widths, are used for simple rod-pocket curtains and valances. Select A. CLEAR OR TRANSLUCENT CURTAIN RODS for lace or sheer curtains, to prevent the rod from showing through and detracting from the fabric. B. WIDE RODS, available in both 2½" (6.5 cm) and 4½" (11.5 cm) widths, add interest to rod-pocket window treatments.

C. DOUBLE CURTAIN RODS consist of two rods with different projections mounted on the same bracket. When curtains and valances are used on a window, the inner rod is used for the curtain and the outer rod for the valance.

Pole sets, including D. CONTEMPORARY METAL, E. TRADITIONAL BRASS, and F. WOOD SETS, are available in several styles and finishes. Unfinished wood pole sets can be painted or stained, using any decorative technique.

How to install hardware using plastic anchors

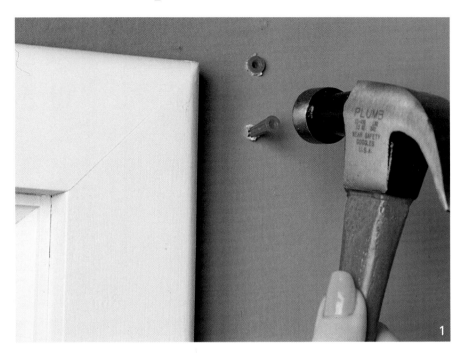

1. Mark the screw locations on the wall. Drill holes for the plastic anchors, using a drill bit slightly smaller than the diameter of the plastic anchor. Tap the plastic anchors into the drilled holes, using a hammer.

2. Insert the screw through the hole in the hardware and into installed plastic anchor. Tighten the screw securely; the anchor expands in drywall, preventing it from pulling out of the wall.

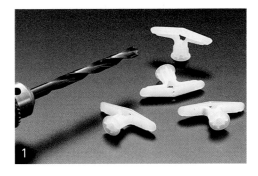

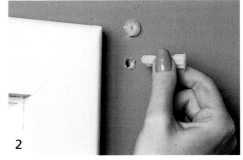

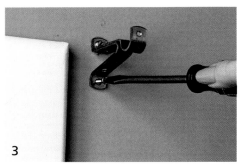

How to install hardware using plastic toggle anchors

1. Mark screw locations on wall. Drill holes for plastic toggle anchors, using drill bit slightly smaller than diameter of toggle anchor shank.

2. Squeeze the wings of the toggle anchor flat, and push toggle anchor into hole; tap in with hammer until it is flush with wall.

3. Insert the screw through hole in hardware and into installed anchor; tighten screw. Wings spread out and flatten against back side of drywall.

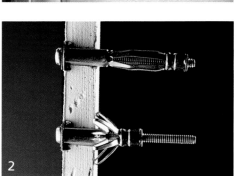

How to install hardware using molly bolts

1. Mark screw locations on wall. Drill holes for molly bolts, using drill bit slightly smaller than diameter of the molly bolt.

2. Tap the molly bolt into the drilled hole, using hammer; tighten screw. Molly bolt expands and flattens against the back side of drywall.

3. Remove screw from molly bolt; insert the screw through hole in hardware and into installed molly bolt. Screw hardware securely in place.

Installing Mounting Boards

Many window treatments are mounted on boards rather than on drapery hardware. The mounting board is covered with fabric to match the window treatment or with drapery lining, and the window treatment is then stapled to the board. The mounting board can be installed as an outside mount, securing it directly to the window frame or to the wall above and outside the window frame. Or the board may be installed as an inside mount by securing it inside the window frame.

The size of the mounting board varies, depending on whether the board-mounted window treatment is an inside or outside mount and whether it is being used alone or with an undertreatment. When using stock, or nominal, lumber, keep in mind that the actual measurement differs from the nominal measurement. A 1 × 2 board measures ¾" × 1½" (2 × 3.8 cm), a 1 × 4 measures ¾" × 3½" (2 × 9 cm), a 1 × 6 measures ¾" × 5½" (2 × 14 cm), and a 1 × 8 measures ¾" × 7¼" (2 × 18.7 cm).

For an inside-mounted window treatment, the depth of the window frame must be at least 1½" (3.8 cm), to accommodate a 1 × 2 mounting board. Cut the mounting board ½" (1.3 cm) shorter than the inside measurement across the window frame, to ensure that the board will fit inside the frame after it is covered with fabric.

The projection necessary for outside-mounted top treatments depends on the projection of any existing undertreatments. If the undertreatment is stationary, allow at least 2" (5 cm) of clearance between it and the top treatment; if the undertreatment traverses, allow at least 3" (7.5 cm) clearance. If there is no undertreatment or if the undertreatment is mounted inside the window frame, use a 1 × 4 board for the top treatment. Cut the mounting board at least 2" (5 cm) wider than the outside measurement across the window frame. Install the board using angle irons that measure more than one-half the projection of the board.

How to cover the mounting board

CUTTING DIRECTIONS

Cut the fabric to cover the mounting board, with the width of the fabric equal to the distance around the mounting board plus 1" (2.5 cm) and the length of the fabric equal to the length of the mounting board plus 3" (7.5 cm).

1. Center board on wrong side of the fabric. Staple one long edge of fabric to board, placing staples about 8" (20.5 cm) apart; do not staple within 6" (15 cm) of ends. Wrap the fabric around board. Fold under ⅜" (1 cm) on long edge; staple to board, placing staples about 6" (15 cm) apart.

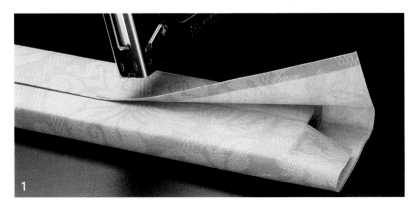

Continued

How to cover the mounting board

(CONTINUED)

2. Miter fabric at corners on side of board with unfolded fabric edge; finger-press. Staple miters in place near raw edge.

3. Miter fabric at corners on side of board with folded fabric edge; finger-press. Fold under excess fabric at ends; staple near fold.

How to install an inside-mounted board

1. Cover the mounting board (above). Attach the window treatment to the mounting board. Hold board in place against upper window frame, with wide side of board up; align front of treatment to front edge of the frame.

2. Predrill screw holes through the board and up into the window frame, using 1/8" drill bit; drill holes within 1" (2.5 cm) of each end of the board and in center for wide window treatments. Adjust placement of holes to avoid screw eyes, if any. Secure the board, using 8 × 1 1/2" (3.8 cm) round-head screws.

How to install an outside-mounted board

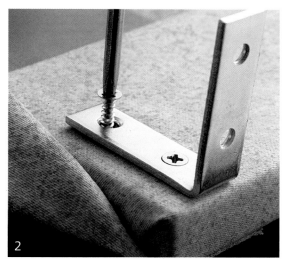

1. Cover mounting board (opposite). Attach window treatment to board. Mark screw holes for angle irons on bottom of board, positioning angle irons within 1" (2.5 cm) of each end of board and at 45" (115 cm) intervals or less; adjust the placement to avoid screw eyes, if any.

2. Predrill screw holes into board; size of drill bit depends on screw size required for angle iron. Screw angle irons to board.

3. Hold board at desired placement, making sure it is level; mark the screw holes on wall or window frame. Remove angle irons from board.

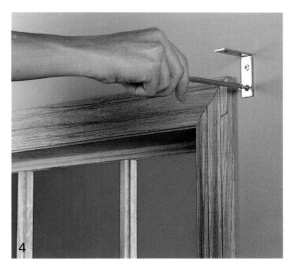

4. Secure angle irons to wall, using 1 1/2" (3.8 cm) flat-heads screws, into wall studs; if angle irons are not positioned at wall studs, use molly bolts or toggle anchors instead of flat-head screws.

5. Reposition window treatment on angle irons, aligning screw holes; fasten screws.

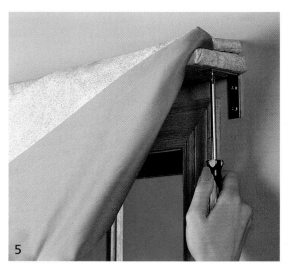

Measuring

Sketch the window treatment to scale on graph paper, to help you determine the most pleasing proportion for the treatment as well as the correct placement of any necessary hardware. After installing the hardware, take all necessary measurements of the window, using a steel tape measure for accuracy, and record the measurements on the sketch.

For each project, you will need to determine the finished length and width of the treatment. The finished length is measured from the top of the mounting board, rod, or heading to where you want the lower edge of the window treatment. The finished width is determined by measuring the length of the rod or mounting board; for treatments with returns, add twice the projection of the rod or mounting board.

Specific instructions for determining the cut lengths and widths of the fabric are given for each project in this book. Yardage requirements can be determined by multiplying the cut length by the number of fabric widths needed to obtain the cut width. When estimating the yardage for patterned fabric, add the length of one pattern repeat for each fabric width needed, to allow for matching the patterns.

TERMS TO KNOW

A. RETURN is the portion of the curtain or top treatment extending from the end of the rod or mounting board to the wall, blocking the side light and view.

B. PROJECTION is the distance the rod or mounting board stands out from the wall. When a wood pole is used, the projection is the distance from the wall to the center of the pole.

C. HEADING is the portion at the top of a rod-pocket curtain that forms a ruffle when the curtain is on the rod. The depth of the heading is the distance from the top of the finished curtain to the top stitching line of the rod pocket.

D. ROD POCKET is the portion of the curtain where the curtain rod is inserted; stitching lines at the top and bottom of the rod pocket keep the rod in place. To determine the depth of the rod pocket, measure around the widest part of the rod or pole; add 1/2" (1.3 cm) ease to this measurement, and divide by two.

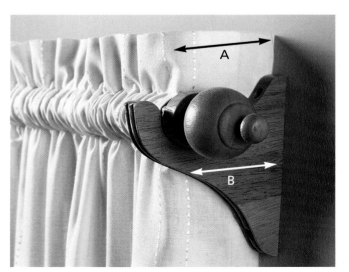

TIPS FOR MEASURING

PLAN the proportion of the layers in a window treatment so the length of the top treatment is about one-fifth the length of the undertreatment. The top treatment may be installed higher than the window, to add visual height to the overall treatment. In some cases, it may be desirable to start the top treatment at the ceiling, provided the top of the window frame is not visible at the lower edge of the top treatment.

PLAN for the shortest point of a top treatment to fall at least 4″ to 6″ (10 to 15 cm) below the top of the window glass. This prevents you from seeing the window frame as you look upward at the top treatment.

ALLOW ½″ (1.3 cm) clearance between the lower edge of the curtain panels and the floor when measuring for floor-length curtains. Allow 1″ (2.5 cm) clearance for loosely woven fabrics, because the curtains may stretch slightly after they are hung.

ALLOW 4″ to 6″ (10 to 15 cm) clearance above baseboard heaters, for safety.

PLAN window treatments to avoid covering heat registers or cold-air returns, for good air circulation.

MEASURE for all curtains in the room to the same height from the floor, for a uniform look. Use the highest window in the room as the standard for measuring the other windows.

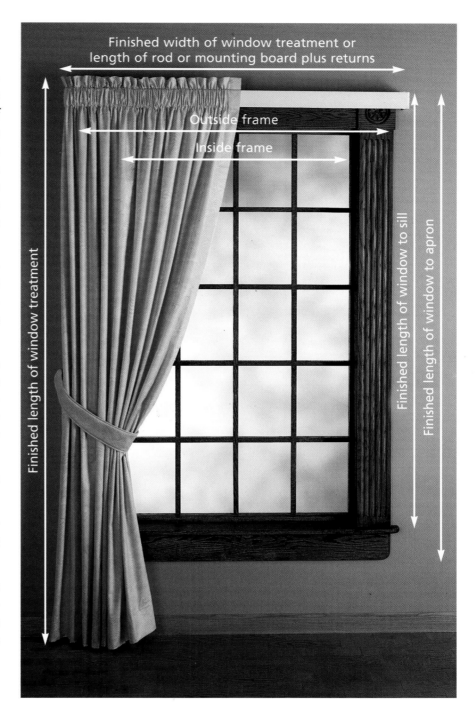

Finished width of window treatment or length of rod or mounting board plus returns

Outside frame

Inside frame

Finished length of window treatment

Finished length of window to sill

Finished length of window to apron

Cutting & Seaming Fabric

When sewing window treatments, a few basic guidelines help ensure good results. The techniques vary somewhat, depending on the type of fabric you are sewing. For any project, it is important to preshrink fabric and lining, using a steam iron, before they are cut.

Many decorator fabrics are tightly woven and may be cut perpendicular to the selvage, using a carpenter's square as a guide for marking the cutting line. However, because lightweight and loosely woven fabrics, such as sheers and casements, tend to slide easily as you cut, it is easier and more accurate to pull a thread along the crosswise grain and cut along the pulled thread.

Patterned decorator fabrics are designed to be matched at the seams (opposite). For window treatments with wide, flat expanses of fabric, it is desirable to eliminate seams by railroading the fabric whenever possible.

Many window treatments look better and are more durable if they are lined. Lining adds body to the treatment as well as protection from sunlight.

TYPES OF SEAMS

A. STRAIGHT-STITCH SEAM, used for lined window treatments, is pressed open.

B. ZIGZAG SEAM, stitched with a narrow zigzag stitch, is used on lace and loosely woven fabrics to prevent puckering; clip the selvages of loosely woven fabrics every 2" (5 cm), allowing the seams to hang smoothly.

C. COMBINATION SEAM, used on tightly woven fabrics, is a straight-stitched seam that is trimmed to 1/4" (6 mm), finished with either an overlock or zigzag stitch, and pressed to one side.

D. FRENCH SEAM is used for sheer fabrics or for window treatments that will be seen from both sides; a narrow seam is first stitched wrong sides together and then stitched again right sides together, encasing the raw edges.

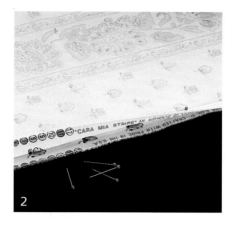

MATCHING PATTERNED FABRICS

1. Position the fabric widths right sides together, matching selvages. Fold back upper selvage until the pattern matches; press foldline.

2. Unfold selvage, and pin the fabric widths together on foldline. Check the match from right side.

3. Repin the fabric so the pins are perpendicular to foldline, stitch on the foldline, using straight stitch.

ROD-MOUNTED VALANCES

*R*od-sleeve Valances

Make quick and easy rod-sleeve valances by simply shirring fabric over a wide curtain rod. Tapered headings are added to the basic rod sleeve to create many different styles. This ruffled top treatment works well over shirred draperies for a feminine look, but may also be used with tailored blinds or pleated shades. The headings may be made from fabric that either matches or contrasts with the fabric for the rod sleeves.

For a dramatic top treatment, two or more curtain rods, covered with basic or tapered-heading rod sleeves, can be grouped together. When two rods are stacked, there is a small space between the rods, due to the mounting brackets. To prevent a light gap, a 1/2" (1.3 cm) extension is added to the lower edge of the upper rod sleeve and tucked behind the lower rod when the top treatment is mounted.

CUTTING DIRECTIONS

For either a basic rod sleeve or a rod sleeve with one heading, the cut length of the sleeve is equal to twice the width of the curtain rod plus 1" (2.5 cm) for ease and 1" (2.5 cm) for seam allowances. To add a 1/2" (1.3 cm) extension between stacked rods, add an extra 1" (2.5 cm) to the cut length. The cut width of the rod sleeve is equal to three times the length of the rod.

If you are making a rod sleeve with two headings, cut separate sections for the front and back of the sleeve, with the cut length of each equal to the width of the rod plus 1" (2.5 cm) for ease and 1" (2.5 cm) for seam allowances. For each front and back, the cut width is equal to three times the length of the rod.

The cut length of a tapered heading is equal to twice the finished length of the heading at the longest point plus 1" (2.5 cm) for seam allowances. The cut width of the heading is the same as the cut width of the rod sleeve.

MATERIALS

- Decorator fabric; one or two fabrics may be used.
- Wide curtain rods, one for each rod sleeve.

TAPERED HEADING sewn at the bottom of the rod sleeve forms a ruffled skirt. A second rod with a basic rod sleeve is stacked above it for a more pronounced effect.

How to sew a basic rod sleeve

1. Seam the fabric widths together. Press seams open. Stitch double ¼" (6 mm) side hems. Fold the rod sleeve in half lengthwise, with right sides together and raw edges even. Sititch ½" (1.3 cm) seam; press open.

2. Turn the rod sleeve right side out; press so the seam is centered on back of sleeve. If extension is required to prevent a light gap on stacked treatment (page 21), stitch ½" (1.3 cm) from the folded edge. Insert curtain rod, gathering fabric evenly.

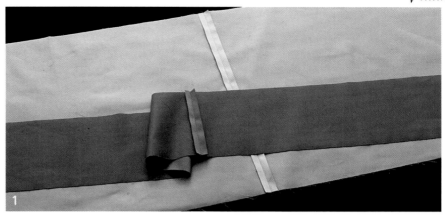

How to sew a rod sleeve with one heading

1. Seam the fabric widths together for rod sleeve and heading. Press seams open.

2. Fold heading in half lengthwise, wrong sides together; press foldline. Then fold in half crosswise; measure from ends a distance equal to twice the depth of return, and pin-mark. For example, for 4″ (10 cm) return, pin-mark 8″ (20.5 cm) from ends.

3. Determine one-third the distance from the pin mark at return to crosswise fold-line; measure this distance from the cross-wise foldline, and pin-mark. This is where tapering will begin.

4. Measure from lengthwise fold at the return pin mark to desired length of head-ing plus ½″ (1.3 cm) seam allowance; mark with pencil. For example, for 4″ (10 cm) heading at return, mark 4½″ (11.5 cm) from lengthwise fold.

Continued

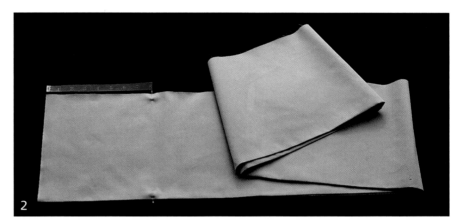

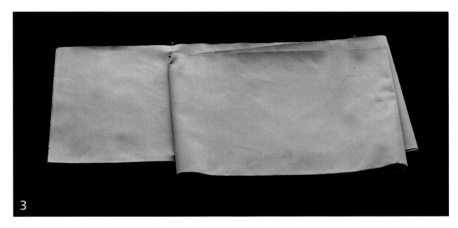

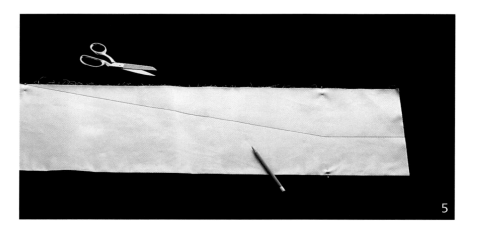

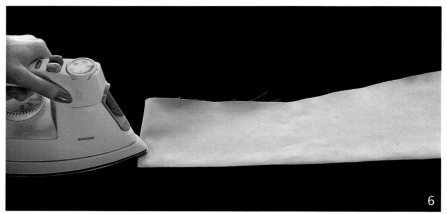

How to sew a rod sleeve with one heading
(CONTINUED)

5. Draw straight line parallel to lengthwise fold, from ends of heading to pencil mark at return. Draw straight line at an angle from pencil mark at return to pin mark in center portion. Cut on marked lines.

6. Fold heading lengthwise, right sides together; stitch 1/2" (1.3 cm) seams at ends. Turn heading right side out; press.

7. Stitch double 1/4" (6 mm) side hems on rod sleeve. Fold rod sleeve in half lengthwise, right sides together; sandwich heading in between, matching raw edges. Pin layers together, easing in seam allowances of heading, as necessary, so fabric lies flat. Stitch 1/2" (1.3 cm) seam.

8. Turn right side out; press. If an extension is required to prevent a light gap on stacked treatment (page 21), stitch 1/2" (1.3 cm) from folded edge. Insert curtain rod, gathering fabric evenly.

TAPERED HEADINGS are used at both the top and bottom of this rod sleeve for a different look.

How to sew a rod sleeve with two headings

1. Seam fabric widths together for headings and front and back of rod sleeve. Press seams open. Make two headings as on pages 23 and 24, steps 2 to 6. Stitch double ¼" (6 mm) side hems in front and back of rod sleeve.

2. Place front and back of rod sleeve right sides together; sandwich headings in between, matching raw edges. Pin layers together, easing in seam allowances of headings as necessary, so fabric lies flat. Stitch ½" (1.3 cm) seams. Turn right side out; press. Insert curtain rod, gathering fabric evenly.

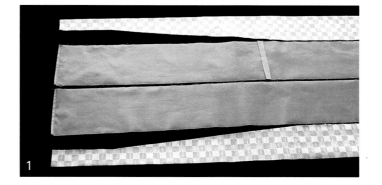

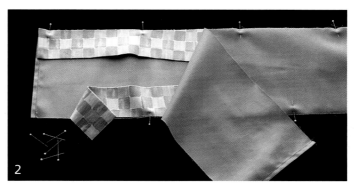

Tapered Valances

Tapered valances frame the window with the graceful lines of a gentle curve. For a simple, no-fuss window treatment, they are often used with blinds or pleated shades. The valance cascades down the sides of the window, showing off the contrasting lining. Ruffles added to the lower edge of a tapered valance give it a country flair.

CUTTING DIRECTIONS

Determine the depth of the rod pocket and heading (page 14). To determine the cut length of the valance and lining panels, measure from the bottom of the rod to the desired length at the side; then add two times the depth of the rod pocket and heading plus 1" (2.5 cm) for seam allowance and turn-under. The cut width of the valance and lining panels is equal to the desired finished width multiplied by two-and-one-half times fullness.

To determine the cut length for the center portion of the valance, add two times the depth of the rod pocket and heading plus 1" (2.5 cm) for seam allowance and turn-under to the desired finished length at the center. This measurement is needed in step 1.

MATERIALS

- Decorator fabric, for valance and lining; contrast fabric may be used for lining.
- Curtain rod.

How to sew a tapered valance

1. Seam fabric widths, if necessary. Divide and mark the width of the valance panel into thirds, using chalk. Fold in half cross-wise; mark cut length for center portion from fold to one-third marking. Measure and mark depth of the return at side (arrow). Draw straight line from return mark to one-third marking at center length.

2. Round upper corner at one-third marking and lower corner at return. Pin fabric layers together; cut along marked lines, following markings for rounded corners. Cut lining panel, using valance panel as a pattern.

3. Pin the valance and lining panels right sides together. Stitch around side and lower edges in ½" (1.3 cm) seam, leaving upper edge open.

4. Press lining seam allowance toward lining. Clip seam allowances at curves, and trim corners diagonally at returns.

5. Turn valance right side out; press seamed edges. Press under ½" (1.3 cm) on the upper edge, folding both layers as one; then press under an amount equal to rod-pocket depth plus heading depth. Stitch close to first fold. Stitch again at depth of heading, using tape on bed of machine as stitching guide.

6. Insert curtain rod through rod pocket, gathering fabric evenly. Install rod on brackets.

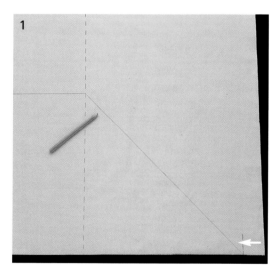

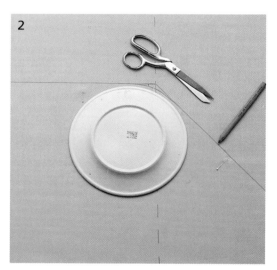

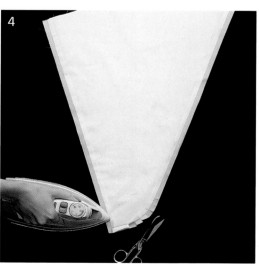

How to sew a ruffled tapered valance

MATERIALS

- Decorator fabric.
- Lining fabric.
- Curtain rod or pole set.
- Cord, such as pearl cotton, for gathering.

CUTTING DIRECTIONS

Cut the valance and lining panels as on page 27. For the ruffle, cut fabric strips two times the finished width of ruffle plus 1" (2.5 cm) for seam allowances. The combined length of the fabric strips is equal to two-and-one-half times the measurement along curved edge of the valance.

1. Prepare valance and lining panels as on page 28, steps 1 and 2. Stitch fabric strips for ruffle together in 1/4" (6 mm) seam, right sides together. Fold pieced strip in half lengthwise, right sides together; stitch across ends in 1/4" (6 mm) seam. Turn right side out; press.

2. Zigzag over a cord within seam allowance of ruffle, just beyond seamline. Zigzag over a second cord 1/4" (6 mm) from first cord, if desired, for more control when adjusting gathers.

3. Divide ruffle and curved edges of valance and lining panels into fourths or eighths; pin-mark, placing pins at sides of valance and lining panels 1/2" (1.3 cm) from raw edges. Place ruffle along curved edge of valance panel, right sides together, matching raw edges and pin marks; pull gathering threads to fit between pins. Machine-baste ruffle, leaving pin marks in place.

4. Place the valance and lining panels right sides together, matching pin marks. Stitch around side and lower edges in 1/2" (1.3 cm) seam, leaving upper edge open. Finish the valance as on page 28, steps 4 to 6.

Vent Hose Cornices

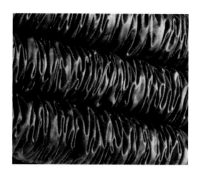

Duplicate the look of designer hardware by using a vent hose, available at hardware stores. Cover the hose with fabric, and insert a curtain rod into the hose for a quick, contemporary cornice. A single covered hose may be used, or for a more substantial cornice, use two or three stacked over each other.

For the cornice, use a curtain rod with a 5" (12.5 cm) projection. If the cornice is mounted over another window treatment, mount the undertreatment on a rod with a 2" (5 cm) projection. This allows for sufficient clearance between the undertreatment and the cornice; the vent hose itself takes up 1 1/2" (3.8 cm) of the clearance between the rods. For clearance at the sides of an undertreatment, mount the curtain rod for the cornice 2" (5 cm) beyond the rod for the undertreatment. If the cornice is used alone, mount the cornice rod 2" (5 cm) beyond the window frame.

CUTTING DIRECTIONS

Stretch the vent hose slightly, and cut it to the length of the curtain rod, including returns; allow slack for going around the returns and for a loosely scrunched look. Cut a strip of fabric 11 1/2" (29.3 cm) wide and two to three times the length of the rod; fabric strip may be pieced, if necessary.

MATERIALS

- ◆ Decorator fabric.
- ◆ 3" (7.5 cm) flexible vinyl vent hose.
- ◆ Curtain rod with 5" (12.5 cm) projection.
- ◆ Masking tape or white tape.
- ◆ Two 1/2" (1.3 cm) cup hooks.

How to make a cornice from vent hose

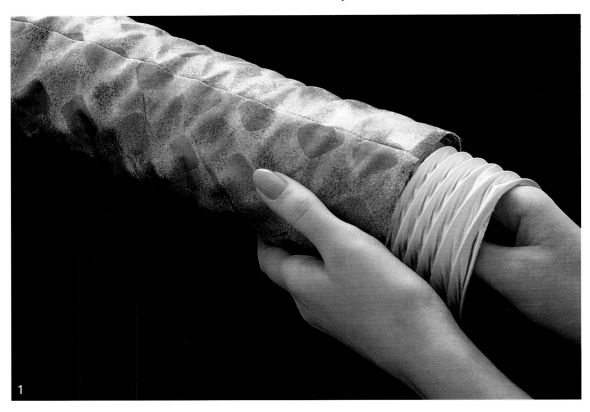

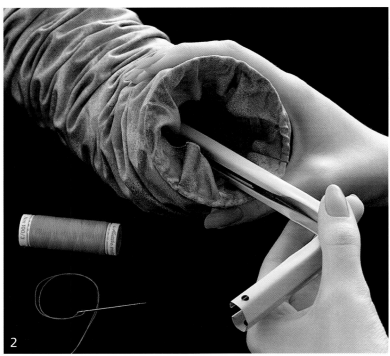

1. Seam the fabric strips together as necessary. Fold strip in half lengthwise, right sides together; stitch 1/4" (6 mm) seam. Turn right side out, and press. Wrap tape around end of wire in vent hose. Slide fabric tube onto vent hose, leaving 1" (2.5 cm) of fabric extending beyond ends of hose; adjust fullness.

2. Fold ends of fabric tube to inside of the vent hose; hand-stitch in place, making sure to catch a row of wire. Insert curtain rod into the covered hose.

3

3. Install brackets (page 8), and mount rod. With top of covered hose resting on curtain rod, position hose against wall at return; mark wall lightly at side of hose.

4. Screw cup hook into wall at mark. Secure covered hose on cup hook, puncturing vinyl; this holds hose flush against wall.

5. Form sharp corners, if desired, by compressing covered vent hose; glue fabric in place at corners, using hot glue.

4

5

Triangle-point Valances

Add a finishing touch over simple window treatments with decorative triangle-point valances. Hung from rings or decorative hooks, the valance falls into gentle folds. The look can vary, depending on the amount of fullness used. Opposite, the valance has about one-and-one-fourth times fullness.

To create a contrasting band of color along the lower and side edges of the valance, add a flat trim, such as grosgrain ribbon or braid. For more elegance, also add a button and tassel to each point of the valance.

CUTTING DIRECTIONS

Determine the desired finished length of the valance at the longest points; to determine the cut length of each fabric width, add 2½" (6.5 cm) to this length. Decide on the approximate fullness of the valance, no more than two times the finished width. Multiply the desired finished width of the valance times the desired fullness; divide this amount by the width of the fabric to determine the number of fabric widths required.

From the decorator fabric and the lining, cut the necessary number of fabric widths, making sure all crosswise cuts are at right angles to the selvage. Make a template for cutting the fabric as on page 36, steps 1 to 4. Using the template, cut the points at the lower edges of the decorator fabric and lining as on page 37, steps 5 to 7.

MATERIALS

- Decorator fabric and lining, 48" or 54" (122 or 137 cm) wide; allow ⅝ yd. to ¾ yd. (0.6 to 0.7 m) for each fabric width needed.
- Grosgrain ribbon, decorative braid, or other tightly woven flat trim;

allow 3 yd. to 4 yd. (2.75 to 3.7 m) for each fabric width needed.
- Decorator pole.
- Clip-on or sew-on drapery rings or decorative hooks.

How to make a triangle-point valance

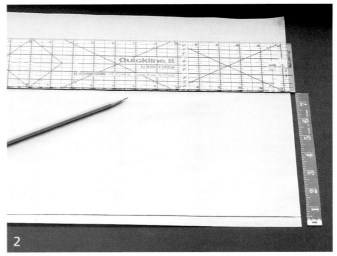

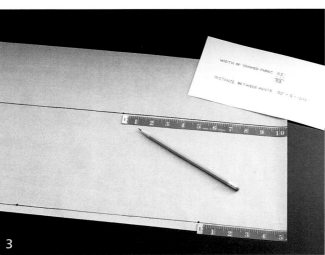

1. Trim the selvages from fabric. Measure the width of trimmed fabric; subtract 1″ (2.5 cm), to allow for ½″ (1.3 cm) seams on each side. To determine distance between lower points of valance, divide this measurement by five; this allows for five lower points per fabric width.

2. Cut a strip of paper, at least 10″ (25.5 cm) long, with width of paper equal to the width of fabric minus seam allowances. Draw two lines across the strip, ½″ (1.3 cm) and 7½″ (19.3 cm) from lower edge.

3. Mark upper angles of points on the upper line, spaced the distance apart determined in step 1. Mark the points of valance along the lower line the same distance apart, starting one-half the distance from edge.

4. Draw lines between the upper and lower points as shown. Add ½″ (1.3 cm) seam allowances at lower edge of the valance. Cut the template.

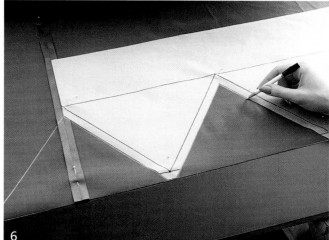

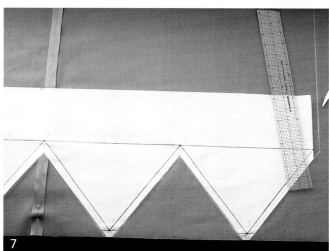

5. Seam the fabric widths. Place the decorator fabric on the lining, right sides together, matching raw edges. Place the template over the first width, with bottom of template along lower edge of fabric; place one end of template 1/2" (1.3 cm) from the raw edge of the fabric and the other end on the seamline. Mark cutting line for lower edge of valance on the fabric.

6. Reposition template on next fabric width, with both ends of template on seamlines; mark lower edge. Repeat for all widths.

7. Cut partial width of fabric as shown, positioning the template with one of the upper points on seamline. Mark 1/2" (1.3 cm) seam allowance beyond the end of the template. Cut the valance and lining along marked lines; transfer the marked points from the template to the fabric. Pin layers together.

8. Sew 1/2" (1.3 cm) seam around sides and lower edge of valance, pivoting at points; leave the upper edge open. Trim the seam allowances at lower points, and clip at upper points. Press lining seam allowance toward lining. Turn valance right side out; press along seamed edges. If the valance does not have trim, omit steps 9 to 11.

Continued

How to make a triangle-point valance

(CONTINUED)

9. Preshrink grosgrain ribbon or braid trim by steam pressing it. Pin trim to one side of valance, with the end of the trim at the upper edge; match outer edges of trim and valance. Pivot trim at lower corner. Mark both edges for miter.

10. Continue to pin trim to lower edge and remaining side of valance; mark both edges for miters at the inner and outer points. Remove trim; stitch and press the miters.

11. Repin trim to the valance. Edgestitch outer edge of trim around the sides and lower edge of valance, from upper edge on one side to the upper edge on opposite side. Edgestitch around the inner edge.

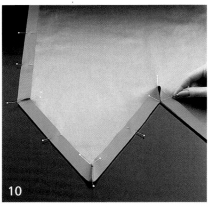

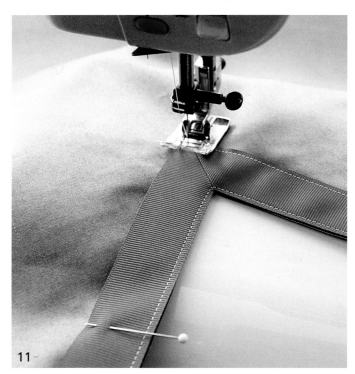

12

12. Press under 1″ (2.5 cm) twice on upper edge, folding both layers as one; stitch close to fold.

13. Attach the rings or decorative hooks to the upper edge of the valance, positioning one at each end and one directly above each of the upper points.

14. Sew a button at each point and attach a tassel, if desired. If the loop on tassel is not large enough to go around the button, sew through loop when attaching button.

15. Hang the valance on decorator pole. Arrange valance for the desired drape between rings. Keep the rings from shifting, using floral adhesive clay or poster putty inside rings, along the top.

13

14

15

Awning Valances

The classic style of an awning valance gives the look of a bistro to a traditional kitchen. Its simple lines also make this window treatment suitable for other decorating styles, including contemporary, transitional, and country.

The main body of the awning is constructed from one or more fabric widths with separate pieces for the rod pockets. Although the length of the awning may vary, a suitable length for most windows is 15" (38 cm).

The awning is supported by two curtain rods of equal length. If the awning is used between wall cabinets, a pressure rod is used for the upper rod. Otherwise, a cafe rod is used for the upper rod; to provide a flush mount, the cafe rod is mounted with cup hooks instead of the usual brackets. For the lower rod, a canopy rod with an 8" (20.5 cm) projection is used, to hold the awning away from the window at the bottom.

CUTTING DIRECTIONS

Make the awning pattern as on page 42, steps 1 to 4; cut one awning piece from the outer fabric and one from the lining. For the upper rod pocket, cut one 3¼" (8.2 cm) strip from the outer fabric, with the length of the strip 2" (5 cm) longer than the rod width measurement from step 1. For the lower rod pocket, cut a 2" (5 cm) strip from the lining fabric; the strip is cut to the same width as the lower edge of the awning pattern.

MATERIALS

- Decorator fabric, for awning and lining.
- Cafe rod, 1" (2.5 cm) cup hooks, and plastic anchors sized for #4 screws, for upper rod if awning is not mounted between wall cabinets. Or pressure rod, for upper rod if awning is mounted between wall cabinets.
- Canopy rod with 8" (20.5 cm) projection, #4 screws, and plastic anchors sized for #4 screws, for lower rod.
- Drill and ⁵/₃₂" drill bit.

How to mount the rods for an awning valance

1. CAFE ROD. Mark position for cup hooks about 1" (2.5 cm) outside and above window frame. Unless at wall stud, drill holes for plastic anchors, using ⁵/₃₂" drill bit. Tap plastic anchors into drilled holes; screw cup hooks into anchors. Repeat to install cup hooks at 36" (91.5 cm) intervals. Hang cafe rod on cup hooks. Mount lower rod after awning is sewn.

2. PRESSURE ROD. Mount a pressure rod between cabinets at top of window, following manufacturer's directions. Mount lower rod after awning is sewn.

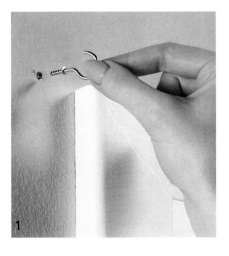

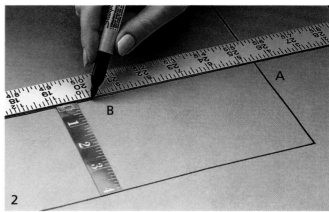

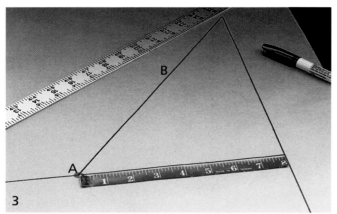

How to make the pattern for an awning valance

1. Measure distance between outer cup hooks or the distance between the wall cabinets; this is rod width measurement. On tracing paper, draw a line for the lower edge of awning equal to rod width plus 16" (40.5 cm).

2. Draw perpendicular line (A) at each end of lower edge, equal to desired length of awning; 15" (38 cm) length works well for most windows. Mark a line (B) across width of pattern, 4" (10 cm) above lower edge; this is the drop length.

3. Mark a dot (A) on marked line for the drop length, 8" (20.5 cm) from side; this marks the point of dart. Draw line (B) from marked dot diagonally to upper end of line for awning length. Repeat for opposite side. Measure length of diagonal line.

4. Draw vertical lines (A) of same length as diagonal lines, starting at marked dots. Draw horizontal line (B) across top of valance; this should measure same distance as rod width. Add ½" (1.3 cm) seam allowances on all sides.

5. Cut one awning piece from outer fabric and one from lining, seaming fabric widths as necessary. Transfer markings for dart points to wrong sides of the outer fabric and lining. Transfer line for drop length to the right side of lining.

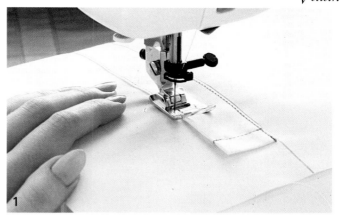

How to sew an awning valance

1. Press ¼" (6 mm) to wrong side on both long edges of lining strip for lower rod pocket. Turn under ½" (1.3 cm) twice at ends; stitch. Pin strip to lining, with top of strip along the marked line for drop length and ends of strip 1" (2.5 cm) from the side edges. Stitch close to top and bottom of strip.

2. Stitch darts in outer fabric, ½" (1.3 cm) from raw edges, stitching to marked dots. Clip to point of each dart, and trim seam allowances near points; press darts open. Repeat for darts in the lining.

3. Press 1" (2.5 cm) to wrong side at each end of the fabric strip for rod pocket; topstitch in place. Fold fabric strip in half lengthwise, wrong sides together; baste raw edges together.

4. Pin rod pocket to upper edge of the awning piece from outer fabric, with the ends of rod pocket at dart seamlines and the raw edges aligned. Stitch ½" (1.3 cm) seam.

5. Pin outer fabric and lining right sides together; stitch around all edges, leaving 5" (12.5 cm) opening along side. Clip corners. Press lining seam allowances toward lining.

6. Turn the awning right side out; press seamline of rod pocket and edges of awning. Slipstitch opening closed. Fold and press awning along dart seamlines, right side out.

7. Insert rods into rod pockets. Hang awning from upper rod. Mark bracket positions for the lower rod, directly under cup hooks or ends of pressure rod. Install lower rod.

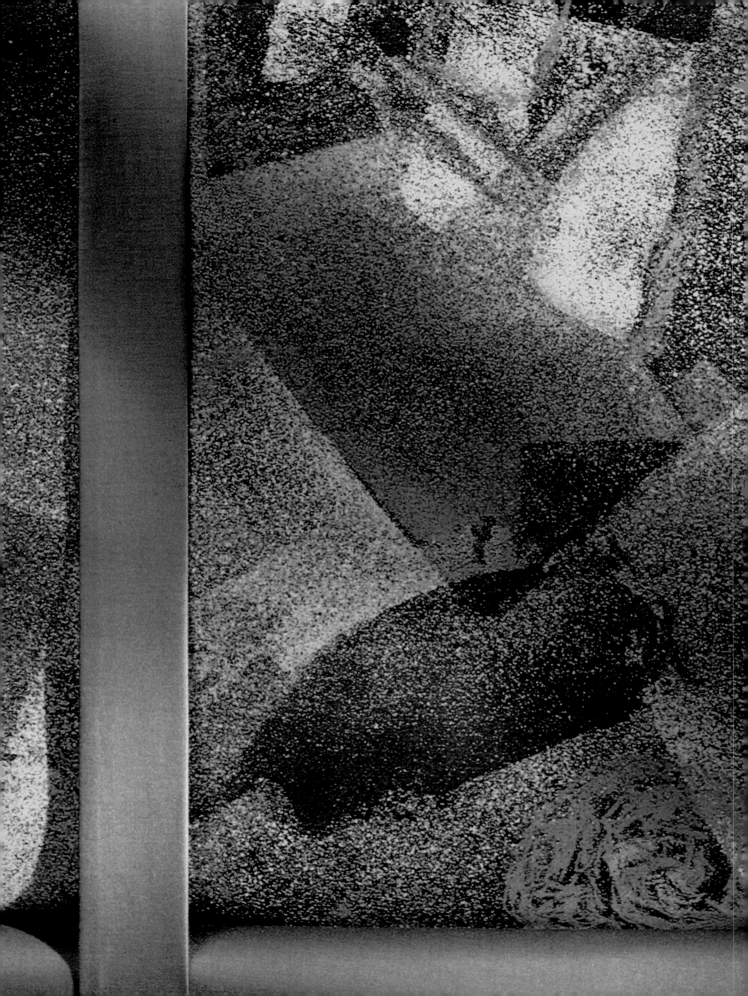

BOARD-MOUNTED VALANCES

CUTTING DIRECTIONS

The cut width of the outer fabric is equal to the length of the mounting board plus two times the finished length of the valance plus 1" (2.5 cm) for seam allowances. The fabric may be railroaded if the design is not directional. Fabric that cannot be railroaded will require piecing if the cut width of the valance is wider than the fabric width; when the fabric is pieced, add the necessary extra width for seam allowances. To determine the cut length of the outer fabric, add the width of the mounting board to the desired finished length of the valance; then subtract 2" (5 cm) from this measurement to allow for seam allowances and for a 3" (7.5 cm) contrasting band at the lower edge.

Cut the contrasting lining the same width as the outer fabric. To determine the cut length of the lining, add the width of the mounting board to the desired finished length of the valance; then add 4" (10 cm) to this measurement to allow for seam allowances and for a 3" (7.5 cm) contrasting band at the lower edge.

Cut fabric to cover the mounting board (page 11).

*H*andkerchief *Valances*

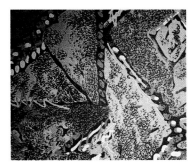

This easy, tailored valance features a 3" (7.5 cm) band at the lower edge, which is simply an extension of the contrasting lining. The valance can be used alone or over another window treatment, such as blinds or underdraperies. It works well for small windows, without being overpowering, but this banded styling is also attractive on larger windows.

A handkerchief valance should be mounted as an outside mount (page 13). The board can either be mounted at the top of the window frame or on the wall above the window. The finished width of the valance should be at least 2" (5 cm) wider than the outside measurement of the window frame or under-treatment; the finished width does not include the fabric drop at the sides of the valance.

MATERIALS

- Decorator fabric in two contrasting colors for outer fabric and lining.
- Mounting board, cut to the desired finished width of valance. Mounting board must be at least 2" (5 cm) wider than projection of window frame or undertreatment.
- Angle irons, one for each end and one for every 45" (115 cm) interval across the width of the mounting board.
- Heavy-duty stapler; staples.
- Pan-head screws or molly bolts (page 10).

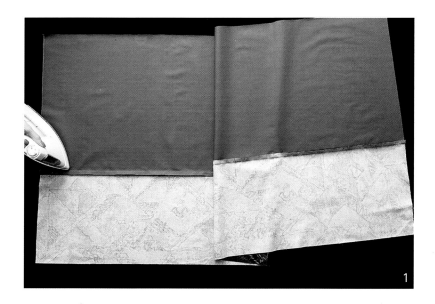

How to sew a handkerchief valance

1. Seam the fabric widths, if necessary. Place the outer fabric and lining right sides together, matching the lower edges; stitch ½" (1.3 cm) seam. Press the seam toward the outer fabric.

2. Place outer fabric and lining right sides together, matching upper edges. Stitch ½" (1.3 cm) seams at the sides and upper edge; leave an 8" (20.5 cm) opening at center of upper edge for turning. Trim the corners diagonally. Press the seam allowances open at edges.

3. Turn the valance right side out. Press edges, folding in seam allowances at the center opening.

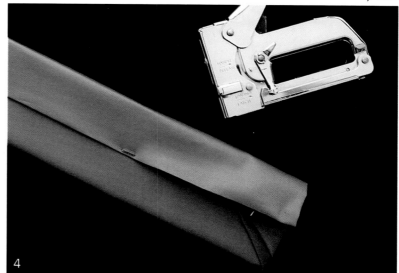

4. Cover mounting board with fabric (page 11); staple the fabric in place at 4" (10 cm) intervals, folding under raw edges.

5. Mark center of mounting board; mark center of valance at upper edge. Place the valance, right side up, on mounting board, aligning upper edge of valance to back edge of board; match center markings. Near the back edge, staple valance to board at center. Working from center to sides, staple valance to the board at 4" (10 cm) intervals, with one staple close to each end.

6. Screw angle irons to bottom of mounting board, positioning one at each end and spacing them at 45" (115 cm) intervals. Install valance on window frame or wall (pages 11 to 13). Adjust the drape at the ends of valance.

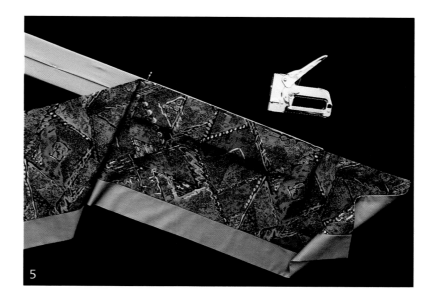

ABOVE: STAGECOACH VALANCE is mounted outside the window frame. Decorative finials are attached to the ends of the PVC pipe that supports the fabric roll at the lower edge of the valance.

RIGHT: INSIDE-MOUNTED STAGE-COACH VALANCE is mounted flush with the front of the window frame, and the ends of the pipe are capped with fabric.

*S*tagecoach Valances

Stagecoaches of the Old West were often fitted with simple shades that were rolled up from the bottom and tied in place. A variation of this shade can be sewn to make a unique stationary valance.

The lower edge of the valance is rolled around a length of PVC plastic pipe, exposing the matching or contrasting lining, and tied with straps of fabric to give the illusion of an operating shade. If a patterned lining is used or if the lining is darker than the valance fabric, interline the treatment to prevent the lining from showing through to the front of the valance when light shines through the window.

The stagecoach valance is attached to a mounting board and can be installed inside or outside the window frame. When installed inside the frame, the ends of the PVC pipe are covered with matching fabric. For an outside mount, returns are added to the sides of the valance above the roll, and finials can be attached to the ends of the pipe.

Space the straps 24" to 36" (61 to 91.5 cm) apart, with the outer straps equal distances from the sides of the valance. For a valance that is wider than the fabric width, railroad the fabric to eliminate the need for seams. If railroading is not possible, try to plan the placement of the seams to fall under the straps.

MATERIALS

- ◆ Decorator fabric, for valance and covered mounting board.
- ◆ Matching or contrasting fabric, for lining.
- ◆ Contrasting fabric, for straps.
- ◆ Drapery lining, for interlining, if necessary.
- ◆ 1 1/4" (3.2 cm) PVC pipe, cut to finished width of valance.
- ◆ Finials designed to fit 1 3/8" (3.5 cm) wood pole and industrial-strength adhesive, for outside-mounted valance, optional.
- ◆ 1 × 2 mounting board for inside mount, length as determined on page 11.
- ◆ Mounting board for outside mount, length and width determined as on page 11.
- ◆ Angle irons with flat-head screws, for installing an outside-mounted valance, with length of angle irons more than one-half the projection of the board.
- ◆ 8 × 2 1/2" (6.5 cm) flat-head screws, for installing an outside-mounted valance into wall studs; or molly bolts or toggle anchors, for installing outside-mounted valance into drywall or plaster.
- ◆ 8 × 1 1/2" (3.8 cm) round-head screws, for installing an inside-mounted valance.
- ◆ Masking tape; staple gun and staples.
- ◆ Drill and 1/8" drill bit.

CUTTING DIRECTIONS

Determine the finished length and width of the valance. For an inside-mounted valance, the width is ¼" (6 mm) less than the inside measurement of the window frame. For an outside-mounted valance, the finished width must be at least 1½" (3.8 cm) wider than the outside measurement of the frame, to allow the necessary space to mount the angle irons at the sides of the frame.

Cut the fabric for the valance with the length equal to the desired finished length of the valance plus 1½" (3.8 cm) for mounting plus 12" (30.5 cm) to roll onto the PVC pipe at the lower edge plus ½" (1.3 cm) seam allowance. For an inside-mounted valance, the cut width of the fabric is equal to the finished width of the valance plus 1" (2.5 cm) for seam allowances. For an outside-mounted valance, the cut width of the fabric is equal to the finished width of the valance plus twice the projection of the mounting board plus ½" (1.3 cm) for seam allowances.

Cut the lining fabric to the same length and width as the valance fabric. Also cut the interlining, if desired, to the same length and width as the valance fabric. For each strap, cut two fabric strips the entire width of the fabric, with the width of each strip equal to twice the desired finished width of the strap plus ½" (1.3 cm) for seam allowances.

Cut the fabric to cover the mounting board (page 11).

How to sew an inside-mounted stagecoach valance

1. Seam fabric widths together, if necessary. Pin the interlining, if desired, to wrong side of the valance fabric; stitch to the valance fabric ⅜" (1 cm) from all edges. Pin valance fabric and lining fabric right sides together, matching the raw edges.

2. Stitch ½" (1.3 cm) seam around sides and lower edge. Trim seam allowances at lower corners diagonally. Press the lining seam allowance toward lining.

3. Turn valance right side out; press seamed edges. Finish upper edge of valance, using overlock or zigzag stitch.

6. Center the pipe on right side of valance at lower edge; tape in place, aligning the lower edge of valance to the marked line on pipe, using masking tape.

7. Roll up the valance to desired finished length. Anchor pipe in place with pins.

8. Fold fabric strips for straps in half lengthwise, right sides together. Stitch long edge and one short end, using ¼" (6 mm) seam allowance. Trim across corners diagonally, turn strap right side out, and press. Two straps are used at each placement.

9. Mark desired placement of the straps at upper edge of valance. Cover the mounting board (page 11); staple valance to the board, lapping upper edge of valance 1½" (3.8 cm) onto the top of board. Do not place staples at markings for straps.

4. Cut two 3" (7.5 cm) circles of decorator fabric. On wrong side, trace the circumference of pipe at center of each circle. Clip at ½" (1.3 cm) intervals from the outer edge to the inner marked circle. Glue to ends of PVC pipe, using craft glue.

5. Hold the pipe firmly in place on a table; place a marker flat on the table and slide it down the length of the pipe, to mark line down center of pipe.

Continued

How to sew an inside-mounted stagecoach valance
(CONTINUED)

10. Sandwich valance between two straps at placement marks; tack in place, using pushpins. Tie finished ends; adjust length of straps from the upper edge, for desired effect, making sure all straps are the same length. Staple straps to board. Trim excess straps at top.

11. Mount the valance (page 11). Hand-tack rolled fabric to the front straps, catching only the back layer of fabric on straps. Remove pins that anchor valance to pipe.

How to sew an outside-mounted stagecoach valance

1. Seam the fabric widths together, if necessary. Fold the fabric in half crosswise, right sides together. At raw edge opposite the fold, mark a distance 12½" (31.8 cm) up from lower edge.

2. Draw a line in from the side at mark, parallel to lower edge, with the length equal to the depth of return. Draw a connecting line, parallel to side, down to lower edge; cut out the section through both layers. The width at the lower edge should now be the finished width of valance plus 1" (2.5 cm).

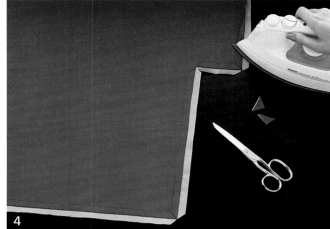

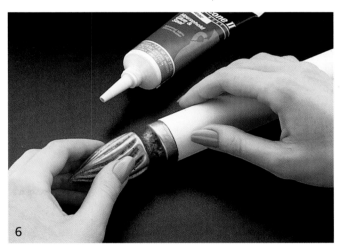

3. Repeat step 2 for lining, and for inter-lining, if used. Pin the interlining, if used, to the wrong side of valance fabric; stitch 3/8" (1 cm) from all sides.

4. Pin valance fabric and lining fabric right sides together, matching raw edges. Stitch 1/2" (1.3 cm) seam around sides and lower edge. Clip and trim corners. Press lining seam allowances toward lining.

5. Turn the valance right side out; press seamed edges. Finish the upper edge of the valance, using overlock or zigzag stitch. Press returns lightly.

6. Cover the ends of the pipe with fabric, if desired, as on page 53, step 4. Or, for pipe with finials, sand ends of pipe smooth; glue the finials to ends of pipe, using industrial-strength adhesive. Follow steps 5 to 8 on page 53.

7. Mark desired placement of the straps at upper edge of valance. Mark the top of mounting board 1 1/2" (3.8 cm) from front edge. Staple valance to covered mounting board (page 11), aligning the upper edge of valance to marked line and with the returns extending at the ends of the board. Do not place staples at markings for straps.

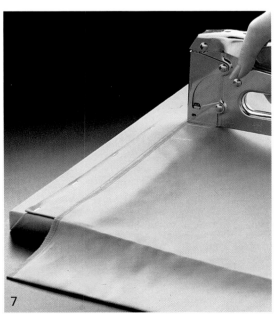

8. Miter the corners of the returns; staple in place. Finish the valance as in steps 10 and 11, opposite.

MATERIALS

- Decorator fabric, for main valance fabric.

- Contrasting decorator fabric, for the pleat inserts.

- Lining fabric, for the interlining, if a light-weight or light-colored patterned fabric is used for valance or inserts.

- Covered buttons or decorative buttons in the desired size; one button is needed for each corner that will be folded back.

- Mounting board, cut to length as determined on page 11.

- Angle irons with flat-head screws; length of angle iron should be more than one-half the projection of board.

- 8 × 2 1/2" (6.5 cm) flat-head screws for installing valance into wall studs; or molly bolts or toggle anchors for installing into drywall or plaster.

- Staple gun and staples.

BUTTONED VALANCES have many design options. The look can be varied, as shown in the examples above, by changing the spacing between the pleats and the way the pleats are folded back.

Buttoned Valances

Box-pleated valances give window treatments the look of tailored simplicity. With the lower corners of the pleats buttoned back, the contrasting fabric of the pleat inserts is revealed. These valances are self-lined, eliminating the need for a lower hem. If the valance or the insert fabric is patterned and either lightweight or light in color, the valance should be interlined with lining fabric.

Pleats are positioned at the outer front corners of the valance. If the projection of the mounting board is less than 5" (12.5 cm), the pleats are not buttoned back on the return sides of the corners. The number of remaining pleats and the spaces between them varies, depending on the size of the window, the desired valance length, and other design considerations. In some cases, it may be desirable to align pleats with existing divisions in the window space created by moldings or mullions, as shown in the diagram at right.

When planning the number of pleats and the spacing, also consider the fabric you are using. You may want to repeat a large motif in each space between the pleats, or perhaps a series of stripes. In general, a fabric with a solid color or a small all-over print can be divided into smaller spaces than a fabric with a large print. The wider the spaces and the larger the print, the more massive the valance will appear.

CALCULATING THE SPACES & PLEATS

Determine the finished width, length, and projection of the valance (page 14). It is helpful to diagram the window treatment. The spaces between the pleats should be at least 10" (25.5 cm) to allow enough room for them to button back. For a valance with evenly spaced pleats, determine the width of the spaces. To do this, first divide the approximate desired space measurement into the width of the valance, rounding up or down to the nearest whole number; this is the number of spaces between the pleats. Divide this number into the valance width to determine the exact measurement of each space. Including the pleats at the outer front corners, there will be one more pleat in the valance than the number of spaces.

MAKING A DIAGRAM. Diagram the window treatment, including any undertreatments. Label the finished length and width of the valance. Plan the placement of the buttoned pleats, with a pleat at each corner. Label the exact width of each space. Label the depth of the return.

From the main valance fabric, cut the fabric for each space section with the cut width equal to the finished width of the space plus 1" (2.5 cm) for seam allowances; the cut length is equal to twice the finished length of the valance plus 3" (7.5 cm) for mounting.

From the main valance fabric, cut the fabric for each return section with the cut width equal to the projection of the mounting board plus 1" (2.5 cm); the cut length is equal to twice the finished length of the valance plus 3" (7.5 cm).

If the projection of the mounting board is more than 5" (12.5 cm), cut the contrasting fabric for all the pleat inserts 21" (53.5 cm) wide, with the cut length of the inserts equal to twice the finished length of the valance plus 3" (7.5 cm).

If the projection of the mounting board is less than 5" (12.5 cm), cut the contrasting fabric for the two corner pleat inserts with the cut width of each insert equal to twice the projection of the mounting board plus 11" (28 cm). For each remaining pleat insert, cut the contrasting fabric 21" (53.5 cm) wide. The cut length of all the pleat inserts is equal to twice the finished length of the valance plus 3" (7.5 cm).

If interlining is desired, the cut width of the lining fabric is equal to the total width of the valance after the valance seams are stitched. The cut length of the lining fabric is equal to the finished length of the valance plus 1 1/2" (3.8 cm).

Cut the fabric to cover the mounting board (page 11).

How to sew a valance with buttoned pleats

1. Pin the pleat insert for left end of the valance over the left return section, right sides together; stitch 1/2" (1.3 cm) seam.

2. Pin a space section to the pleat insert, right sides together; stitch 1/2" (1.3 cm) seam. Continue to join sections, alternating pleat inserts and space sections; end with the right pleat insert and the right return section. Press seams open.

3. Fold the end of the valance in half lengthwise, right sides together. Sew 1/2" (1.3 cm) seam on outer edge of return; turn valance right side out, and press. Repeat for the opposite end of valance.

4. Press the valance in half, matching raw edges and seams. Machine-baste the layers together, 1/2" (1.3 cm) from raw edges at top of valance.

5. Mark center of each pleat insert along upper and lower edges. If return is less than 5" (12.5 cm), measure from inner seam of return a distance equal to twice the return; pin-mark.

6. Fold under pleats at all seamlines; press. Bring the pressed seams together to pin marks; pin pleats in place along upper and lower edges.

Continued

How to sew a valance with buttoned pleats

(CONTINUED)

7. Press folded edges of all pleats, turning the valance back and pressing only on the pleat, to avoid imprinting edges to right side of valance.

8. Stitch pleats in place across the valance, 1½" (3.8 cm) from upper edge. Finish the upper edge, using overlock or zigzag stitch.

9. Fold back lower corners of pleats at desired angle to expose pleat insert. Pin in place; press, if desired.

10. Determine button placement. Sew the buttons in place through all layers. For shank-style buttons, cut a small slit in the fabric, through corner layers only. Insert the shank through the slit; sew the button through remaining layers.

11. Cover the mounting board (page 11). Position valance on the mounting board, using the stitching line as guide to extend the upper edge 1½" (3.8 cm) onto top of board; position end pleats at the front corners of board. Clip the fabric at corner pleats close to the stitching line. Staple the valance in place, beginning with returns; ease or stretch valance slightly to fit board, if necessary. Mount the valance (page 11).

How to sew an interlined valance with buttoned pleats

1. Follow steps 1 and 2, page 58; measure the width of seamed valance. For interlining, cut the lining fabric to this measurement, seaming widths together as necessary. Pin interlining to wrong side of valance, matching upper edges and ends.

2. Complete the valance as in steps 3 to 11, pages 59 and 60. The lower edge of interlining extends to the lower fold of valance.

Index

CY DECOSSE INCORPORATED

President/COO: Nino Tarantino
Executive V.P./Editor-in-Chief: William B. Jones
Chairman Emeritus: Cy DeCosse

Creative Touches™
Group Executive Editor: Zoe A. Graul
Managing Editor: Elaine Johnson
Editor: Linda Neubauer
Associate Creative Director: Lisa Rosenthal
Senior Art Director: Delores Swanson
Art Director: Mark Jacobson
Contributing Art Director: Judith Meyers
Copy Editor: Janice Cauley
Desktop Publishing Specialist: Laurie Kristensen
Sample Production Manager: Carol Olson
Studio Manager: Marcia Chambers
Print Production Manager: Patt Sizer

President/COO: Philip L. Penny

VALANCES ETC.
Created by: The Editors of Cy DeCosse Incorporated

Also available in the Creative Touches™ series:

*Stenciling Etc., Sponging Etc., Stone Finishes Etc.,
Painted Designs Etc., Metallic Finishes Etc., Swags Etc.,
Papering Projects Etc.*

The Creative Touches™ series draws from the individual titles of
The Home Decorating Institute®. Individual titles are also available
from the publisher and in bookstores and fabric stores.

Printed on American paper by:
  R. R. Donnelley & Sons Co.
99 98 97 96 / 5 4 3 2 1

Cy DeCosse Incorporated offers a variety of how-to books.

For information write:
  Cy DeCosse Subscriber Books
  5900 Green Oak Drive
  Minnetonka, MN 55343